MW00388036

PACEMAKER®

World Geography and Cultures

WORKBOOK

Douglass/ESOL
New 04

GLOBE FEARON
Pearson Learning Group

Pacemaker® World Geography and Cultures Second Edition

Executive Editor: Jane Petlinski
Lead Editor: Wendy Svec
Editor: Alisa Brightman
Production Editor: Marcela Maslanczuk
Lead Designer: Tricia Battipede
Cover and Interior Designer: April Okano
Electronic Specialists: Leslie Greenberg, Susan Levine
Manufacturing Supervisor: Mark Cirillo

About the Cover: *World Geography and Cultures* is the study of the world and the world's people. The images on the cover are objects that represent the different regions of the world. A mask from Mexico shows the sun, a common theme in Latin America. Money from South Africa includes a drawing of a native animal, the elephant. A ship from Asia, called a junk, is an important mode of travel. A lei from the South Pacific is a necklace woven from fresh flowers. The wooden clogs are shoes from the Netherlands in Europe. Anasazi Indians in the North American Southwest made the decorated pot. What images would represent objects made where you live?

Copyright © 2002 by Pearson Education, Inc., publishing as Globe Fearon, an imprint of Pearson Learning Group, 299 Jefferson Road, Parsippany, New Jersey, 07054. All rights reserved. No part of this book may be reproduced or transmitted in any form or by any means, electronic or mechanical, including photocopying, recording, or by any information storage and retrieval system, without permission in writing from the publisher. For information regarding permission(s), write to Rights and Permissions Department.

ISBN 0-130-23676-4
Printed in the United States of America
 4 5 6 7 8 9 10   05 04 03

1-800-321-3106
www.pearsonlearning.com

Contents

A Note to the Student

The exercises in this workbook go along with your *Pacemaker® World Geography and Cultures* textbook. Each exercise in the workbook is linked to a chapter in your textbook. This workbook gives you the opportunity to do three things—review, practice, and think critically.

The review exercises are questions and activities that test your knowledge of the information presented in the textbook. Set goals for yourself, and try to meet them as you complete each activity. Being able to remember and apply information is an important skill that leads to success in school, at work, and in life.

The skill practice exercises help you to apply geography and social studies skills. You will need these skills as you read and write about the information that you have learned in your textbook. Some pages in the workbook have charts, maps, or graphs. These pages will give you extra practice in using your chart, map, or graph skillls.

Your critical thinking skills are challenged when you complete the critical thinking exercises. Critical thinking—or to put it another way, thinking critically—means putting information to use. For example, you may review and recall information about the different nations that comprise a region. Later you might use that information to explain what happened during a war between those nations. When you apply what you have learned to a new situation, you are thinking critically.

Your textbook is a wonderful source of knowledge. By using it along with this workbook, you will learn a great deal about world geography and cultures. The real value of the information will come when you have mastered the skills and put them to use by thinking critically.

Name _____   Date _____

Match the letters on the globes with the terms below.

The Hemispheres

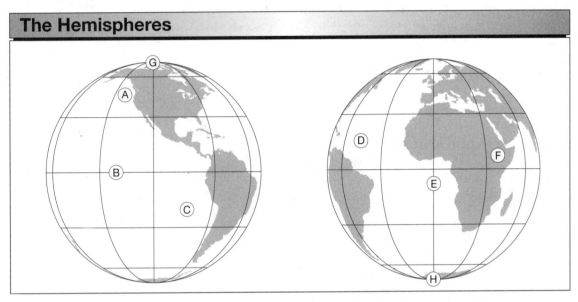

_____ **1.** equator

_____ **2.** Northern Hemisphere

_____ **3.** Southern Hemisphere

_____ **4.** Eastern Hemisphere

_____ **5.** Western Hemisphere

_____ **6.** North Pole

_____ **7.** South Pole

_____ **8.** prime meridian

Copyright © by Pearson Education, Inc. All rights reserved.

Name_____ Date_____

A. Each of the following descriptions belongs under one of the five themes of geography: *location, place, interaction, movement,* or *region.* Write the correct theme beside each description.

  1. Christopher Columbus was just one of the European explorers who reached new lands while searching for shorter trade routes.

  _____

  2. The Canadian city of Montreal is found at approximately 45 degrees N latitude, 76 degrees W longitude. _____

  3. Rain seldom falls in the arid deserts of Arizona. _____

  4. Hardy pioneers moved west across the United States to lands that offered adventure and new opportunities. _____

  5. New Orleans, Louisiana, and Cairo, Egypt, are both found at a latitude of approximately 30 degrees N. _____

  6. The Pilgrims came to America seeking religious freedom.

  _____

  7. Dust storms often sweep the level, almost treeless prairies of North Dakota. _____

  8. Some farmers cut down trees to clear the land for their crops.

  _____

  9. Oregon, Washington, and California are Pacific states.

  _____

  10. A northern area with an extremely cold climate has become known as the Arctic. _____

B. On a separate sheet of paper, write a paragraph describing ways in which people in your region interact with their environment.

Copyright © by Pearson Education, Inc. All rights reserved.

Name _____ Date _____

A. Draw a map of your state showing the *location* of your city.

B. Write a paragraph identifying the *region* in which you live.
How do you define the boundaries of that region? What
common characteristics do parts of your region share?

_____

_____

_____

_____

_____

_____

Copyright © by Pearson Education, Inc. All rights reserved.

Name_____ Date_____

Use information on the map to answer the questions below.

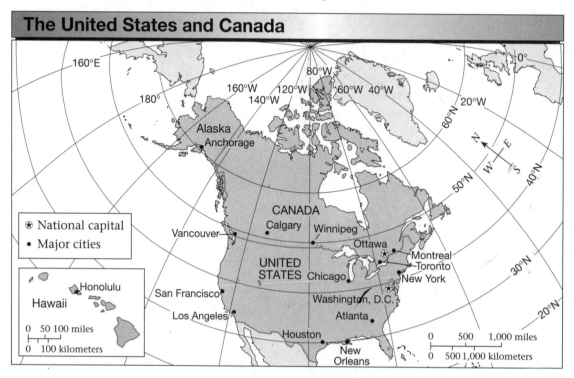

The United States and Canada

1. Which city's latitude on the map is farthest north? _____

2. What city is at about 30°N, 90°W? _____

3. Which city is closer to 120°W, San Francisco or Los Angeles? _____

4. Which three cities are closest to 50°N? _____

   _____

5. New York and Washington, D.C., are closest to what latitude? _____

6. What is the approximate latitude and longitude of Montreal? _____

7. Which national capital is closest to 40°N? _____

8. What is the approximate latitude and longitude of the city on the map

   closest to where you live? _____

Copyright © by Pearson Education, Inc. All rights reserved.

Name _____   Date _____

2 ▸ Classifying Terms   **Exercise 5**

Circle the one item in each group that *does not* belong.

1. seasons of the year:

   summer   spring   January   fall   winter

2. layers of the Earth:

   crust   equator   mantle   core

3. metals in the Earth's core:

   silver   nickel   iron

4. landforms:

   valleys   canyons   plateaus   wind

5. climate:

   temperature   wind patterns   rivers   rainfall

6. factors affecting climate:

   distance from the equator   population

   distance from the ocean   elevation

7. climate regions:

   industrial   polar   tropical   dry

8. natural resources:

   air   automobiles   water   minerals

9. nonrenewable resources:

   oil   coal   gold   trees

10. renewable energy sources:

    solar power   wind power   fossil fuel

Copyright © by Pearson Education, Inc. All rights reserved.

Name_____ Date_____

2 ► Matching Cause and Effect

Exercise 6

Critical Thinking

A. Each action described in the sentences at the left causes an effect described in the sentences at the right. Match each cause with an effect by writing the letter next to the number.

_____ **1.** Activity within the Earth builds heat and pressure.

_____ **2.** Wind and water erode and weather the Earth.

_____ **3.** The Earth moves around the sun.

_____ **4.** The Earth tilts on its axis.

_____ **5.** The Earth spins on its axis.

_____ **6.** The Earth turns 15° an hour.

_____ **7.** Industries use CFCs.

_____ **8.** The hole in the ozone layer gets bigger.

a. This causes a 365-day year.

b. This causes our seasons.

c. This causes movements in the Earth's crusts—earthquakes.

d. This causes damage to the ozone layer.

e. This causes a change in time zones.

f. This causes more ultraviolet rays to pour down on the Earth.

g. This shapes the Earth's surface.

h. This causes a 24-hour day.

B. On a separate sheet of paper, write a letter to the editor of your local newspaper. Explain why you feel it is important that people do one of the following:

• Develop energy sources other than fossil fuels
• Use sunscreen when working or playing outdoors
• Make sure automobiles meet emission standards
• Preserve the Earth's rain forests

Copyright © by Pearson Education, Inc. All rights reserved.

Name _____   Date _____

3 ▷ Categorizing Information   Exercise 7

A. Follow the directions for each item below.

1. Circle each item that could be included in the category of *culture*.

   a. crafts   **c.** clothing   **e.** oceans

   b. houses   **d.** sports   **f.** buildings

2. Circle each item that could be included in the category of *social structures*.

   a. families   **c.** automobiles   **e.** governments

   b. clubs   **d.** teams   **f.** maps

3. Circle each items that could be included in the category of *customs*.

   a. religious ceremonies   **c.** dress   **e.** table manners

   b. diet   **d.** holiday celebrations   **f.** landforms

B. Compare the customs of your culture with those of another country. Choose one of the items below to compare.

- rituals of marriage and weddings
- the celebration of a major spring holiday
- rituals of death and burial
- the celebration of a major winter holiday
- dress

_____

_____

_____

_____

_____

_____

_____

_____

_____

Copyright © by Pearson Education, Inc. All rights reserved.

Name _____ Date _____

Critical Thinking

In Chapter 3, you read how the houses people build reflect the places they live (the physical geography) and the way they live (the human geography). Think about a type of housing typical in your region. Then, answer each of the following.

1. Where do you live? _____

2. Write two or three sentences describing a type of housing typical of your region.

    _____

    _____

    _____

    _____

3. What kind of building material is often used? How does the choice of material reflect characteristics of your region?

    _____

    _____

    _____

    _____

4. What special features make the house suitable to the climate of your region?

    _____

    _____

    _____

    _____

5. How does the house reflect the way people in your region live?

    _____

    _____

6. On a separate sheet of paper, sketch the type of house you have described.

Copyright © by Pearson Education, Inc. All rights reserved.

Name _____ Date _____

 3 ▶ **Using a Chart**   **Exercise 9**

A. Use information from the chart to list the countries in order of
their population densities. Country number 1 should have the
lowest population density. Country number 12 should have the
highest. Number one has been filled in for you.

Population Density and Distribution of Selected Countries of the World		
Country	**Population Density**	**Urban Population**
China	337 per square mile	29%
Canada	8 per square mile	77%
Sweden	51 per square mile	83%
U.S.A.	73 per square mile	76%
France	279 per square mile	74%
Germany	596 per square mile	87%
Japan	865 per square mile	78%
Bolivia	19 per square mile	61%
Mexico	132 per square mile	74%
India	789 per square mile	27%
Russia	22 per square mile	76%
Nigeria	319 per square mile	40%

Source: *The World Almanac,* 2000

1. *Canada* _____   **5.** _____   **9.** _____

2. _____   **6.** _____   **10.** _____

3. _____   **7.** _____   **11.** _____

4. _____   **8.** _____   **12.** _____

B. Create *pie graphs* that represent the urban populations in two
of the countries listed on the chart. A pie graph representing
Canada has been done as an example.

77%
Urban

Canada

_____   _____   _____

Copyright © by Pearson Education, Inc. All rights reserved.

Name _____ Date _____

4 ▸ Classifying Information

A. Each of the following statements describes the geography of the
United States or Canada or both. Decide whether each statement
belongs under the category of *landforms, climate, human features,* or
economy. Write one category on the line following each statement.

1. A flat, rolling area called the Coastal Plain stretches down the Atlantic Coast.

   _____

2. The United States and Canada are rich countries in comparison with many

   nations of the world. _____

3. Both the United States and Canada are democracies. _____

4. The Rocky Mountains start in Alaska and run almost to the Mexican border.

   _____

5. The Pacific Northwest gets fog and drizzle about half of the year. _____

6. The Southwest is the driest part of the United States. _____

7. Both the United States and Canada profit from the export of wheat.

   _____

8. The majority of people in Canada and the United States speak English.

   _____

9. People of the United States and Canada follow many different religions.

   _____

10. The St. Lawrence River marks part of the border between the United

    States and Canada. _____

B. On a separate sheet of paper, compare a city in the United States
with a city in Canada. Include location, a brief history, population,
major industries, and cultural events. Research the cities on the
Internet to find up-to-date information.

Copyright © by Pearson Education, Inc. All rights reserved.

Name _____   Date _____

Use information on the map to answer the questions below.

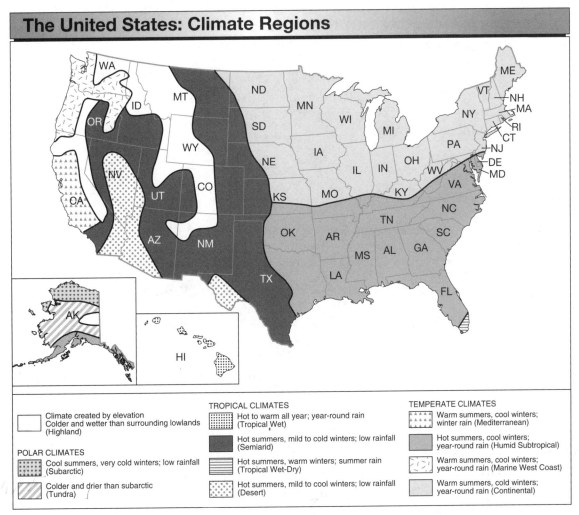

The United States: Climate Regions

Climate created by elevation
Colder and wetter than surrounding lowlands
(Highland)

POLAR CLIMATES
Cool summers, very cold winters; low rainfall
(Subarctic)

Colder and drier than subarctic
(Tundra)

TROPICAL CLIMATES
Hot to warm all year; year-round rain
(Tropical Wet)

Hot summers, mild to cold winters; low rainfall
(Semiarid)

Hot summers, warm winters; summer rain
(Tropical Wet-Dry)

Hot summers, mild to cool winters; low rainfall
(Desert)

TEMPERATE CLIMATES
Warm summers, cool winters;
winter rain (Mediterranean)

Hot summers, cool winters;
year-round rain (Humid Subtropical)

Warm summers, cool winters;
year-round rain (Marine West Coast)

Warm summers, cold winters;
year-round rain (Continental)

1. How does the map describe the climate of your region? _____

_____

2. Which state has a *tropical wet* climate? _____

3. Which state has a *polar* or *subarctic* climate? _____

4. What type of climate would you find along the Pacific Northwest coast?

_____

5. If you are traveling to Hawaii, would you be wise to pack an umbrella?

_____

Copyright © by Pearson Education, Inc. All rights reserved.

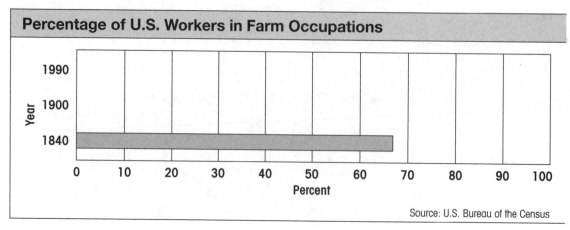

4 ▸ Understanding Point of View

A. Point of view is a certain way of looking at a situation. Point of view is determined by one's past experiences and personal interests. For example, a lumber company executive would probably have different views about logging practices than an environmentalist. Read and answer the questions below.

1. A debate is being held over logging restrictions in an old-growth forest. Write a statement from the point of view of a representative of a large lumber company.

_____

_____

_____

_____

2. Now write a statement from an environmentalist's point of view.

_____

_____

_____

_____

B. In 1840, approximately 69 percent of U.S. workers were employed in farm occupations. In 1900, 37.5 percent worked in farm occupations. In 1990, 1.6 percent of the workers were employed in farm occupations. Complete the following *bar graph* by adding bars to represent 1900 and 1990. On a separate sheet of paper, write a conclusion based on the information in the bar graph.

Percentage of U.S. Workers in Farm Occupations

Year: 1990, 1900, 1840

Percent: 0 10 20 30 40 50 60 70 80 90 100

Source: U.S. Bureau of the Census

Copyright © by Pearson Education, Inc. All rights reserved.

Name _____   Date _____

A. Complete the information on the chart below. Refer to Chapter 5
in your textbook if you need help. The first one has been
completed as an example.

Select Early Native American Groups			
Native American Group	**Region (Where lived)**	**Housing**	**Way of Life**
Iroquois	Northeast forests	longhouses	hunters and farmers
Sioux			
Pueblo			
Kwakiutl			
Inuit			

B. If you were a member of one of the Native American groups
above, what would a diary entry for a day in your life be?
Write one below.

_____

_____

_____

_____

_____

_____

_____

_____

_____

_____

_____

Copyright © by Pearson Education, Inc. All rights reserved.

Name _____ Date _____

A. Write the following events in the order in which they occurred.

    a. In 1492, Christopher Columbus landed on an island near Florida and called the people who were living there "Indians."

    b. The early Americans spread out across North and South America, branching into different groups.

    c. The very first Americans came to North America from Asia across a land bridge.

    d. In 1968, Native Americans founded the American Indian Movement (AIM) to promote their culture.

    e. In 1944, Native Americans formed a political organization called the National Congress of American Indians.

    f. In 1910, the Native American population began to rise again.

    g. European settlers brought diseases that killed many Native Americans.

    1. _____

    2. _____

    3. _____

    4. _____

    5. _____

    6. _____

    7. _____

B. Choose one of the events above, and write a paragraph that includes three important details about that event.

_____

_____

_____

_____

_____

_____

Copyright © by Pearson Education, Inc. All rights reserved.

Name _____ Date _____

A. A *fact* is a statement that can be proved true or false. An *opinion* tells
what someone believes about something. A statement of opinion often
shows approval or disapproval. It cannot be proved either true or false.
Decide whether each statement is a fact or an opinion. Write *F* or *O*
beside each statement.

_____ **1.** After European settlers arrived in America, they started killing buffalo.

_____ **2.** The Iroquois lived in large wooden houses called longhouses.

_____ **3.** The Canadian government should not have interfered with the Inuit
way of life.

_____ **4.** United States President Andrew Jackson was cruel to force the
American Indians off their southeastern lands.

_____ **5.** The Inuit and Aleut lived in cold, northern regions.

_____ **6.** The Inuit and Aleut would have found life easier in warmer,
southern lands.

_____ **7.** Organizations like AIM are good ways for Native Americans to gain
political strength and preserve their culture.

_____ **8.** A Sioux community in the Central Plains runs a pencil company.

_____ **9.** A powwow is a celebration of Native American culture.

_____ **10.** An American Indian powwow is a fascinating event.

B. Write one statement of fact that you learned about Native Americans
while reading Chapter 5. Write one statement of opinion that you
formed after reading Chapter 5.

_____

_____

_____

_____

Copyright © by Pearson Education, Inc. All rights reserved.

6 ▸ Conducting an Interview

Exercise 16

Critical Thinking

A. Interview people in your school, and make a list of their ethnic backgrounds. Then, write a sentence or two identifying the major ethnic backgrounds.

_____

_____

_____

_____

_____

_____

_____

B. Write a summary of a recent news story involving immigrants.

_____

_____

_____

_____

_____

C. Look through a city newspaper or a magazine or on the Internet for announcements of ethnic festivals, recipes for ethnic foods, or advertisements for ethnic restaurants in your area. Share your findings with the class.

Copyright © by Pearson Education, Inc. All rights reserved.

6 ▶ Describing the Life of an Immigrant

Exercise 17

Critical Thinking

You have just immigrated to the United States from another country. Write a letter to a friend in your homeland. Describe your new life in the United States, your hopes for the future, your problems, and your daily adventures. Contrast it to what your life was like in your homeland.

_____

_____

_____

_____

_____

_____

_____

_____

_____

_____

_____

_____

_____

_____

_____

_____

_____

_____

_____

_____

Copyright © by Pearson Education, Inc. All rights reserved.

6 ▶ Recognizing the Main Idea

Exercise 18

Review

A. The main idea is the most important idea in a paragraph. It tells what the paragraph is about. A sentence that gives the main idea does not list individual details. It presents the main point those details would support. Circle the letter of the sentence that presents the *main idea* of each topic.

1. The separatist movement in Québec

   a. There are French-speaking people who want to separate Québec from Canada.

   b. Many people in Québec speak French.

   c. Some people in Québec speak English.

2. The celebration of Kwanzaa

   a. Kwanzaa runs from December 26 to January 1.

   b. African Americans celebrate a harvest holiday called Kwanzaa.

   c. One day of Kwanzaa is set aside to honor the principle of "working together."

3. African Americans today

   a. African Americans helped build the economy of the south.

   b. African American folk tales have become apart of American folklore.

   c. African Americans have deeply affected American culture.

4. Ethnic influence in the southwestern United States

   a. Many buildings have tile roofs similar to those in Spain and Mexico.

   b. The southwestern United States shows a strong Hispanic influence.

   c. In 1835, Texas broke away from Mexico.

B. When you compare things, you tell how they are alike. When you contrast them, you tell how they are different. On a separate sheet of paper, contrast how the first Africans came to the United States with how the first European immigrants came.

Copyright © by Pearson Education, Inc. All rights reserved.

Name _____ Date _____

 7 ▷ **Sequencing Events**

A. Rewrite the following events in the order in which they occurred. Use number one for the earliest event.

a. Mexico became free from Spain in 1821.
b. Spanish conquerors destroyed the Aztec civilization in the early 1500s.
c. Mexico City is one of the world's largest cities.
d. The Aztec civilization rose to power during the 1300s.
e. In 1917, a new constitution was written.
f. In 1910, rebels rose up against President Díaz.
g. Porfirio Díaz became president of Mexico in 1876.
h. After the Spaniard Cortéz conquered the Aztecs, Mexico became a colony of Spain.

1. _____

2. _____

3. _____

4. _____

5. _____

6. _____

7. _____

8. _____

B. Use the information listed above to answer these questions.

1. What European country took control of Mexico in the early 1500s? _____

2. When did Mexico win its independence? _____

3. Was Mexico under foreign rule for more or less than 100 years? _____

4. Which Mexican city is one of the largest cities in the world? _____

Copyright © by Pearson Education, Inc. All rights reserved.

7 ▷ Making Comparisons

Exercise 20

Review

Write a sentence for each situation below. Use Chapter 7 if you need help.

1. Compare Mexico City with Washington, D.C.

_____

_____

_____

2. Compare the climate of Mexico's Central Plateau with the climate of southern Mexico.

_____

_____

_____

3. Compare the size of the ancient Aztec capital of Tenochtitlán with the size of London, England.

_____

_____

_____

4. Compare the roles played by Father Hidalgo and Pancho Villa.

_____

_____

_____

5. Compare land ownership in Mexico before and after the Mexican revolution.

_____

_____

_____

Copyright © by Pearson Education, Inc. All rights reserved.

8 ▶ Using a Map   **Exercise 23**

A. Look at the map of Central America on page 103 in your textbook. Use this map to circle the words that correctly complete each sentence.

1. *(United States, Brazil, Mexico)* is Central America's closest northern neighbor.

2. The Panama Canal links the Pacific Ocean with the *(Caribbean Sea, Gulf of Mexico, Atlantic Ocean)*.

3. Panama was the most likely country in which to build a canal because *(it is the only country that borders two seas, it is the narrowest country, it is the closest country to the United States)*.

4. *(Colombia, Mexico, Spain)* is Central America's closest southern neighbor.

5. The ancient Mayan civilization developed in Belize, Honduras, and Guatemala. This means that most of the Maya lived in *(northern, southern)* Central America.

B. Use information from Chapter 8 to write one factual sentence about these Central American nations.

1. Belize: _____

_____

2. Guatemala: _____

_____

3. Honduras: _____

_____

4. El Salvador: _____

_____

5. Nicaragua: _____

_____

Copyright © by Pearson Education, Inc. All rights reserved.

Name _____ Date _____

Use these terms to complete the crossword puzzle.

adobe√	calendar√	Contra√	embroidery√	huipil
Ladinos√	Popul Vuh√	Quiché	rain forest√	Tikal√

Across

1. dense forests like these grow in warm, wet areas near the equator

5. a Mayan sacred book

7. a Mayan invention

8. a Nicaraguan guerrilla soldier who fought the Sandinistas

9. descendants of the ancient Maya

Down

2. dried mud and straw

3. ancient Mayan capital

4. designs stitched into plain fabric

6. Guatemalan mestizos

10. a blouse worn by Mayan women

Copyright © by Pearson Education, Inc. All rights reserved.

9 ▶ Using a Timeline

Exercise 25

Skill Practice

This timeline shows when South American nations gained their independence from European powers. Fill in the blank lines on the map below. Write the name of each country and the year it became independent. The map on page 117 in your textbook can help you to locate the countries.

South American Nations: Dates of Independence

| **1811** Paraguay | **1818** Chile | **1821** Peru | **1825** Bolivia | **1828** Uruguay | **1962** Trinidad and Tobago | **1975** Suriname |

1810 1812 1814 1816 1818 1820 1822 1824 1826 1828 1830 — 1960 1975

| **1816** Argentina | **1819** Colombia | **1822** Brazil | **1830** Venezuela, Ecuador | **1966** Guyana |

South America

French Guiana

Copyright © by Pearson Education, Inc. All rights reserved.

Name _____ Date _____

Write a paragraph describing the Incan civilization. Use at least *five* of the words in the box below. Underline these words when you use them in your paragraph. You might want to use reference works or the Internet for help.

emperor	temples	quipus	Spaniards	terraces
aqueducts	llamas	empire	Andes	earthquakes

_____

_____

_____

_____

_____

_____

_____

_____

_____

_____

_____

_____

_____

_____

_____

_____

_____

_____

Copyright © by Pearson Education, Inc. All rights reserved.

Name_____ Date_____

The map below shows three great civilizations of early Latin America: the
Aztecs of Mexico, the Maya of Central America, and the Incas of Peru.

Early Latin American Civilizations

All of the following statements are false. Change the underlined word in
each sentence to make the statement true. Use information from the map
to rewrite each sentence.

1. The Incas built a great empire in western <u>Mexico</u>.

_____

2. The Incan capital of Cuzco, built high in the <u>Rocky</u> Mountains,
had stone palaces and pyramid-shape temples.

_____

3. The Maya of <u>South America</u> worshiped many gods.

_____

4. The Incan empire stretched over almost all of the <u>Atlantic</u> coast
of South America.

_____

Copyright © by Pearson Education, Inc. All rights reserved.

10 ▶ Categorizing Islands   **Exercise 28**

A. Most Caribbean islands belong to an archipelago called the
Antilles. As you learned in Chapter 10, the four largest islands
are called the *Greater Antilles.* The smaller islands are called
the *Lesser Antilles.* Categorize each of the listed islands under
Greater Antilles or Lesser Antilles. Use the map on page 134
of your textbook and a reference book—such as an almanac
or an encyclopedia—to help you complete this activity.

Barbados	Cuba	Grenada	Hispaniola	Jamaica
Martinique	Puerto Rico	Trinidad	Virgin Islands	

Greater Antilles   **Lesser Antilles**

_____   _____

_____   _____

_____   _____

_____   _____

B. Each term listed in Column A is representative of an island
nation listed in Column B. Match the words in Column A with
the countries in Column B. Write the letter by the number.

A	**B**
_____ **1.** communism	**a.** Puerto Rico
_____ **2.** coral islands	**b.** Hispaniola
_____ **3.** divided into Haiti and the Dominican Republic	**c.** Haiti
_____ **4.** United States commonwealth	**d.** Bahamas
_____ **5.** "Baby Doc" Duvalier	**e.** Cuba

Copyright © by Pearson Education, Inc. All rights reserved.

Name _____   Date _____

By filling in the blanks below with the correct words from the box, you will discover a code. Each number represents the letter above it. Using the code, find the answer to the question at the bottom of the page. One letter has been supplied for you.

| pirates | Virgin Islands | Creole | Caribs | trade winds |

1. These breezes blow southwest from the Atlantic Ocean and cool the Caribbean Islands.

___ ___ ___ ___ ___   ___ ___ ___ ___ ___
 2   1   8   12 20   10   3 11 12   5

2. These daring bandits attacked Spanish ships and stole their gold.

___ ___ ___ ___ ___ ___ ___
 16   3   1   8   2   20   5

3. This language was formed when French mixed with West African languages.

___ ___ ___ ___ ___ ___
 18   1   20   4   17 20

4. This group of tiny islands lies east of Puerto Rico and is part of the Lesser Antilles.

___ ___ ___ ___ ___ ___   ___ ___ ___ ___ ___ ___ ___
 7   3   1   15   3   11   3   5   17   8   11   12   5

5. The entire region and the sea are named after this group of Indians who came from South America.

___ ___ ___ ___ ___ ___
 18   8   1   3   14   5

This is an element of religious life in Haiti. What is it?

___ ___ ___ ___ ___ ___   ___ ___ ___ ___ h ___ ___
 5   16   3   1   3   2   10   4   1   5   3   16

Copyright © by Pearson Education, Inc. All rights reserved.

11 ▶ Comparing Civilizations

A. In Chapter 11, you read about the early civilizations of West Africa. Each of the following descriptions applies to one of these civilizations. Write *G* for the kingdom of Ghana, *M* for the kingdom of Mali, or *S* for the kingdom of Songhai beside each number.

_____ **1.** This civilization rose to power under a group called the Soninke.

_____ **2.** This civilization was ruled by the Malinke group.

_____ **3.** This civilization traded goods for gold and then traded gold for salt.

_____ **4.** Emperors of this civilization made their capital at Timbuktu.

_____ **5.** This civilization conquered others because it had iron weapons.

_____ **6.** This civilization followed the Mali and lasted about 150 years.

B. Choose one of the following essay topics. On a separate sheet of paper, write an essay on the topic you chose.

• Compare the kingdom of Ghana to the kingdom of Mali.
• Compare the way the Ibo and the Hausa dealt with the British colonization of Nigeria.
• Compare the West African civilization before and during the days of slave trade.

Copyright © by Pearson Education, Inc. All rights reserved.

11 ▶ Interpreting a Story

Exercise 31

Critical Thinking

A. West Africans told stories to explain their world and their
religious beliefs. Find the country of Togo on a map of West
Africa. The following story comes from the Krachi people of Togo.
After you read the Krachi story, complete each statement below.

A Higher Sky

Wulbari was the great creator. He was the sky and the heaven. He spread
himself out less than five feet above the Earth's surface.

"Ouch!" cried Wulbari many times every day. For when a man would stand
up, he'd often bump his head against Wulbari. Wulbari thought it was very
rude indeed.

Once, an old woman was pounding grain. She raised her pounding stick,
then smashed it down upon the grain. Each time she raised her stick, she
poked Wulbari right in the eye!

"Ouch!" Wulbari cried. "I had better raise myself up a bit!"

So he did. Yet, he was still quite close to the Earth. People came to know
Wulbari so well that they took him for granted. Children wiped their dirty
hands on the sky. Once someone even tore a piece of blue right out of the
sky to add to a soup.

"I've had enough!" Wulbari finally exclaimed. He rose higher and higher.
He stretched out blue and beautiful out of everyone's reach. So it has been
ever since.

---

1. The story explains why _____

2. Wulbari became angry when an old woman poked him with _____

3. People took Wulbari for granted because _____

4. According to the story, Wulbari can now be found _____

B. On a separate sheet of paper, write an original story explaining
some aspect of your world. You might use one of the following
topics or come up with a topic of your own.

• Why the sky is blue

• Why volcanoes sometimes erupt

• Why the moon shines at night

• Why it snows in winter

Copyright © by Pearson Education, Inc. All rights reserved.

Name _____ Date _____

Use the information from the chart to answer the questions below.

Nigeria: Selected Information	
Population	113,800,000
Population density	319 per square mile
Main ethnic groups	Hausa, Yoruba, Ibo, Fulani
Languages	English (official), Hausa, Yoruba, Ibo
Exports	98 percent crude oil
Finance	$1,300 average per capita Gross Domestic Product (GDP)
Communications	4 television sets per 100 persons
Life expectancy	52 years male, 54 years female
Literacy rate	57 percent

Source: *The World Almanac,* 2000

1. What are the four main ethnic groups in Nigeria today?

_____

2. What product accounts for a large share of Nigeria's income?

_____

3. Notice the statistics on ownership of televisions in Nigeria. What would you guess that statistic to be in the United States?

_____

4. In the United States, the life expectancy is 72, male, and 79, female. What do Nigeria's life expectancy statistics tell you about health care in that country?

_____

5. The United States literacy rate is about 97 percent. What do the literacy statistics tell you about education in Nigeria?

_____

_____

Copyright © by Pearson Education, Inc. All rights reserved.

Name _____ Date _____

1. Describe three *causes* of desertification.

   Cause 1: _____

   _____

   Cause 2: _____

   _____

   Cause 3: _____

   _____

2. Name two of the *effects* of heavy rains in the Democratic Republic of the Congo.

   Effect 1: _____

   _____

   Effect 2: _____

   _____

3. Name two *causes* of tropical disease.

   Cause 1: _____

   _____

   Cause 2: _____

   _____

4. Describe one *effect* that tropical disease has had on Central Africa.

   Effect: _____

   _____

5. Describe one *cause* and one *effect* of the Central African governments' attempts to eliminate tsetse flies.

   Cause: _____

   Effect: _____

Copyright © by Pearson Education, Inc. All rights reserved.

12 ▸ Designing a Brochure

Exercise 34

Critical Thinking

A. You are employed by the Central Africa Bureau of Tourism. You have been asked to design a travel brochure inviting tourists to vacation in Central Africa. Write a paragraph describing features of Central Africa that might attract visitors. On a separate sheet of paper, draw a picture or select magazine photographs to illustrate your brochure.

Central Africa: Land of _____

_____

_____

_____

_____

_____

_____

_____

_____

_____

_____

_____

B. Now, you are planning a trip to Central Africa. List five items you would be sure to pack. Explain why you would include each item.

_____

_____

_____

_____

Copyright © by Pearson Education, Inc. All rights reserved.

12 ▶ Using the Internet

Exercise 35

Critical Thinking

A. The following African animals have been classified as endangered species. Choose one of these animals. On a separate sheet of paper, write a one-page report about the species and its habitat. Explain the threats to its existence. Describe measures being taken to protect the species. You might illustrate your report with original drawings, copies of photographs, or magazine pictures.

Some of Africa's Endangered Species	
Cheetah	Mountain Zebra
Gorilla	Black Rhinoceros

B. There are many endangered species of wild animals and birds within the United States. Use the Internet or reference books from the library to find out what U.S. species are in danger of extinction. Make a list of ten of these species, and tell where they can be found.

_____

_____

_____

_____

_____

_____

_____

_____

_____

Copyright © by Pearson Education, Inc. All rights reserved.

13 ▷ Stating Your Opinion

Exercise 36
Critical Thinking

Read the items below and answer the questions.

1. In 1992, the United States sent troops to Somalia as part of a United States mission to enforce peace and to try to get food to starving people in Somalia. Do you think the United States should use military force to protect and aid civilians in other nations? Give reasons for your opinion. Describe another time when the United States sent military aid to another nation.

_____

_____

_____

_____

_____

_____

_____

2. Preserving and protecting wildlife can be difficult. As populations grow, people need more land. They sometimes compete with animals for limited resources. In certain cases, people destroy wildlife in an attempt to earn a living. Do you think humans should be asked to sacrifice jobs and economic stability in an effort to preserve a species? Explain your answer.

_____

_____

_____

_____

_____

_____

Copyright © by Pearson Education, Inc. All rights reserved.

Name _____ Date _____

A. Use the following chart to compare the nations of East Africa.
Circle each correct answer below.

Nation	Approximate population	Population density (per sq. mi.)	Area (sq. mi.)	Chief crop and industry	Literacy rate	Problems (1990–2000)
Ethiopia	59,680,383	137	435,185	coffee	35%	drought, hunger, unstable government
Somalia	7,140,643	29	246,200	incense sugar	24%	unstable government, hunger
Djibouti	447,439	53	8,500	salt	46%	unemployment, few natural resources
Uganda	22,804,973	250	91,000	coffee cotton	62%	disputes with neighboring Tanzania, economic woes
Kenya	28,808,658	128	225,000	coffee corn tourism	78%	ethnic group conflicts
Tanzania	31,270,820	86	364,900	sisal cotton	68%	disputes with Uganda

Source: *The World Almanac,* 2000

1. *(Ethiopia, Kenya)* has the larger area.

2. More than half of the people in *(Ethiopia, Uganda)* can read.

3. Kenya and Ethiopia are similar in *(size, population density)*.

4. There have been conflicts between *(Somalia and Ethiopia, Tanzania and Uganda)*.

5. The nation of *(Tanzania, Djibouti)* has the higher literacy rate.

B. Review the section in Chapter 13 titled "Marriage Customs."
On a separate sheet of paper, write a paragraph contrasting
African marriage customs with those in the United States.

Copyright © by Pearson Education, Inc. All rights reserved.

Name _____ Date _____

This map shows the nations of southern Africa. Use the map and information from Chapter 14 to answer the questions and complete the activities. You will need colored pens, pencils, or crayons.

1. Which southern African nation is an island in the Indian Ocean?

   _____ Color that nation red.

2. Which two countries are at least partly surrounded by South Africa?

   _____ and _____
   Color those two nations purple.

3. Which nation is the most highly industrialized?

   _____ Color that nation green.

4. In which nation would you find the capital city of Gaborone?

   _____ Color that nation brown.

5. In which nation would you find ruins of a great Bantu city?

   _____ Color that nation yellow.

Copyright © by Pearson Education, Inc. All rights reserved.

Copyright © by Pearson Education, Inc. All rights reserved.

Name _____ Date _____

14 ▸ Sequencing Events

A. You can find the dates of each of the following events in Chapter 14. Write the date on the line after each event.

a. F. W. de Klerk is elected president of South Africa. (date: _____)

b. South African government rules that all blacks must become citizens of

a "homeland." (date: _____)

c. Afrikaners' political party wins control of South Africa in all-white election.

(date: _____)

d. African National Congress (ANC) leader Nelson Mandela is released from prison.

(date: _____)

e. Black leaders in South Africa form the ANC. (date: _____)

f. ANC leader Nelson Mandela is arrested. (date: _____)

B. Describe the South Africa you predict will exist in the year 2020. Write a paragraph including answers to at least three of these questions:

• What group or groups hold power?
• Has South Africa become a peaceful land?
• What is South Africa's relationship with nations in the rest of the world?
• Does the legacy of apartheid linger? Why or why not?
• How is Afrikaner rule remembered?

_____

_____

_____

_____

_____

_____

_____

Name _____ Date _____

Unscramble the names of the North African countries. Then, write
them in the correct locations on the map below.

Countries of North Africa

G E L A I R A = _____

Y A B L I = _____

R O O M C O C = _____

S U N I T I A = _____

T Y P E G = _____

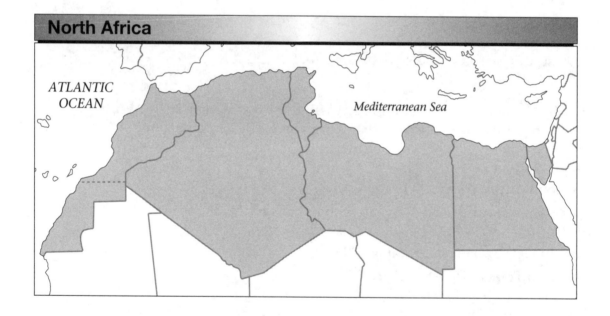

North Africa

ATLANTIC OCEAN

Mediterranean Sea

Copyright © by Pearson Education, Inc. All rights reserved.

15 ▷ Classifying Terms

A. Cross out one item in each group that *does not* belong.

1. Countries of North Africa:

Morocco   Algeria   Turkey   Tunisia   Libya   Egypt

2. Main languages spoken in North Africa:

Arabic   Berber   English

3. Ways that Egyptians earn money:

selling oil   selling cotton   mining silver   Suez Canal   tourism

4. Physical features of North Africa:

Atlas Mountains   Sahara   Panama Canal   Nile River valley

5. Developments of the ancient Egyptians:

clocks   pyramids   hieroglyphics   calendar

6. Democratic republics:

Algeria   Tunisia   Egypt   Morocco

B. Certain events have shaped the course of history in North Africa.
Choose one of the events below, and write what might have happened if:

- methods of irrigation had not been invented.
- the Aswan High Dam had never been built.
- Britain had kept control of the Suez Canal.

_____

_____

_____

_____

_____

_____

Copyright © by Pearson Education, Inc. All rights reserved.

Name _____ Date _____

Use information from the chart to answer the questions below.

Country	Major Religion	Government	Per capita Gross Domestic Product	Literacy rate
Algeria	Islam	republic	$4,000	62%
Egypt	Islam	republic	$4,400	51%
Libya	Islam	socialist military dictatorship	$6,700	76%
Morocco	Islam	monarchy	$3,500	44%
Tunisia	Islam	republic	$6,100	67%

Source: *The World Almanac,* 2000

1. In which North African nations can more than half the population read and write?

_____   _____

_____   _____

2. What is the major religion in all the nations listed on the chart?

_____

3. Which nation produced the greatest total value of goods and services?

_____

4. What was the per capita Gross National Product for Algeria?

_____

5. Which nation is governed by a military dictator?

_____

6. In which nation would you expect to find a king at the head of the government?

_____

Copyright © by Pearson Education, Inc. All rights reserved.

Name _____   Date _____

16 ▶ Learning About Agriculture

Exercise 43

Critical Thinking

Find out more information about agriculture in Israel. Use an encyclopedia, an almanac, or the Internet to help answer the following questions.

1. Much of Israel is desert, yet farmers produce about three-fourths of the country's food. Find two ways by which Israelis are able to farm their arid land.

_____

_____

_____

_____

2. Name two of Israel's chief crops.

_____

_____

3. Most Israeli farmers belong to cooperative or collective communities. What is the difference between a cooperative community, called a moshav, and a collective community, called a kibbutz?

_____

_____

_____

_____

_____

_____

4. Find out how much Israel exported in the most recent year recorded. The number should include agricultural products as well as other products. Write the total dollar amount.

_____

Copyright © by Pearson Education, Inc. All rights reserved.

Name_____ Date_____

Write a paragraph describing Islamic countries and traditions. Use at least *five* of the terms from the box. Underline the terms when you use them in your paragraph.

mosque	pilgrimage	alms	fast	veils
Mecca	sharia	Koran	Ramadan	

_____

_____

_____

_____

_____

_____

_____

_____

_____

_____

_____

_____

_____

_____

_____

_____

_____

_____

_____

Copyright © by Pearson Education, Inc. All rights reserved.

Name_____ Date_____

A. The following information describes the approximate amount of crude oil produced by various Middle Eastern countries in 1999. Chart this information on a bar graph. Saudi Arabia has already been graphed as an example.

Iran: 90 billion barrels

Saudi Arabia: 259 billion barrels

Syria: 2.5 billion barrels

Iraq: 112.5 billion barrels

Kuwait: 94 billion barrels

United Arab Emirates: 98 billion barrels

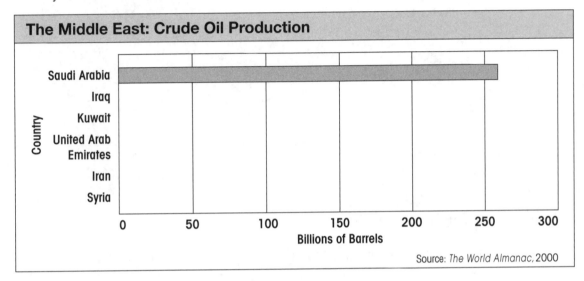

The Middle East: Crude Oil Production

Source: *The World Almanac,* 2000

B. Chapter 16 tells that the conflict between Israelis and Palestinians has yet to be resolved. Find a newspaper or magazine article or an Internet report that describes a recent event in the Israeli-Palestinian conflict. Read the article and write a three-sentence summary.

_____

_____

_____

_____

_____

_____

_____

_____

Copyright © by Pearson Education, Inc. All rights reserved.

17 ▶ Classifying Information

A. Classify each of the following under the heading of *Turkey* or the heading of *Iran*.

secular government	theocracy	mostly Shiite Muslim
mostly Sunnite Muslim	Khomeini	Kemal Ataturk

Turkey   **Iran**

_____   _____

_____   _____

_____   _____

_____   _____

_____   _____

B. Describe the following Middle Eastern leaders.

Describe three ways Ataturk changed life for the people of his country.

1. _____

2. _____

3. _____

Describe three ways Khomeini changed life for the people of his country.

1. _____

2. _____

3. _____

Copyright © by Pearson Education, Inc. All rights reserved.

Name _____   Date _____

Islam is the major religion in Turkey and Iran. It is the major religion
in many other countries as well. The following map shows some of the
countries in Europe, the Middle East, and Africa where most Muslims live.
Use the map to decide if the statements below are true or false. Write *True*
or *False* beside each number.

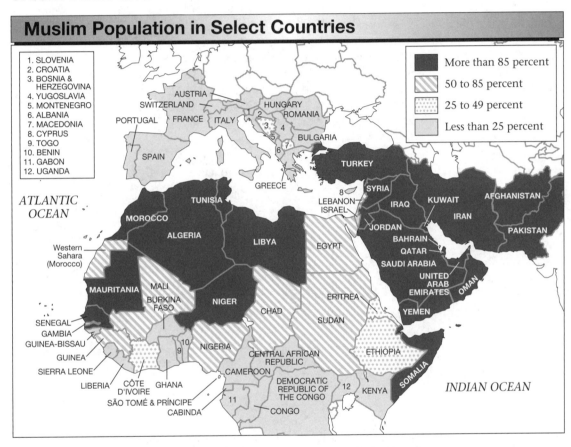

Muslim Population in Select Countries

_____ **1.** More than 85 percent of the populations of Turkey and Iran are Muslim.

_____ **2.** Israel is the only Middle Eastern country with a Muslim minority.

_____ **3.** Muslim populations of over 85 percent can only be found in Africa.

_____ **4.** The Persian Gulf is surrounded by countries with large

Muslim populations.

_____ **5.** Kuwait has a Muslim population of less than 25 percent.

_____ **6.** There are no Muslims living on the continent of Europe.

Copyright © by Pearson Education, Inc. All rights reserved.

Name _____ Date _____

A. Read the following paragraph.

> The countries of the British Isles vary greatly in population and size. Scotland's land area is 30,420 square miles. About 5,128,000 people live there. This is about 169 people per square mile. Wales is about 8,020 square miles. About 2,921,000 people live in Wales, which is about 364 people per square mile. England is the largest country in the British Isles. It is 50,350 square miles. England is also the most densely populated country. About 49,089,000 people live there. This is about 975 people per square mile.
>
> The Republic of Ireland is 27,133 square miles. About 3,619,480 people live there. Its population density is 133 people per square mile. In Northern Ireland, about 1,663,000 people live in a density of about 304 people per square mile. There are about 5,470 square miles in Northern Ireland.

B. Use the information in the above paragraph to complete this chart.

The British Isles			
Country	Area (square miles)	Population	Population density (per square mile)
Northern Ireland	5,470	1,663,000	304
Republic of Ireland			
England			
Scotland			
Wales			

C. Use the information in the above chart to answer the questions below.

1. List the countries from greatest to smallest population.

_____

_____

2. Which country is the largest in size?

_____

2. Which country has the smallest population density?

_____

Copyright © by Pearson Education, Inc. All rights reserved.

18 ▸ Identifying Causes and Results

Exercise 49

Review

A. Three of the following statements describe events that led to the English Industrial Revolution. Put a check mark by those statements.

The Industrial Revolution came about because:

_____ **1.** James Watt invented a new steam engine.

_____ **2.** England had an especially dry summer.

_____ **3.** coal could be used to produce iron.

_____ **4.** England developed a better system of roads and canals.

_____ **5.** William Shakespeare wrote *Romeo and Juliet*.

B. Five of the following statements describe the results of the English Industrial Revolution. Put a check mark by those statements.

Because of the Industrial Revolution:

_____ **1.** more people moved to the cities.

_____ **2.** more people moved to the country.

_____ **3.** the middle class grew more powerful.

_____ **4.** the gap between the rich and the poor widened.

_____ **5.** England had a classless society in which all were equal.

_____ **6.** cities were cleaner and less crowded.

_____ **7.** poor urban areas called slums developed.

_____ **8.** the working class grew.

_____ **9.** working conditions improved for all people.

Copyright © by Pearson Education, Inc. All rights reserved.

18 ▷ Comparing Past and Present

Exercise 50

Skill Practice

A. Read about a Scottish tradition of yesterday and today.

> The Highland Games probably began in the tenth or eleventh century among the clans of Scotland. Clan chiefs brought together their strongest warriors to fight and race against those of other clans. One of the first Highland Games may have been hosted by King Malcolm Canmore. He thought the mail was being delivered too slowly to his castle in the Highlands. He wanted to find strong, swift runners to employ as mail carriers. The prize for the winner was a sword and a bag of gold—and the job of king's runner.
>
> Other competitions later became part of the Highland Games. Tossing the caber was one of these. The caber, which looks like a telephone pole, weighs about 90 pounds and is about 17 feet long. The player threw the caber so that it landed with the small end pointing away from the thrower. The farthest throw won. Another ancient Highland game was the weight-for-height contest. Men competed to see who could throw a 56-pound piece of metal highest. In the weight-for-distance contest, men threw a 28-pound hammer head as far as they could.
>
> Today, Highland Games are still popular in Scotland. Those who compete in these events must wear a kilt. Men still toss the caber and throw the weight for height and distance. There are still plenty of running races in the modern gatherings. There are also contests in long jump, hurdles, and pole vault. More than 40 different Highland Games take place each year in Scotland.

B. Circle the letter of the words that best complete each sentence below.

1. One of the prizes at the Highland Games held by King Malcolm Canmore was

  a. a shield.   **b.** a suit of armor.   **c.** a sword.

2. The caber looks like

  a. a telephone pole.   **b.** a cannonball.   **c.** a baseball bat.

3. An ancient competition from the Highland Games that is still held today is

  a. the weight for height and distance.   **b.** the joust.   **c.** the high bar.

4. Those competing in the caber throw today must

  a. speak Scottish.   **b.** pledge loyalty to the king.   **c.** wear a kilt.

5. One competition you will not find in the modern games is

  a. running races.   **b.** pole vaulting.   **c.** wrestling.

C. On a separate sheet of paper, write an essay about the Highland Games. Discuss why and how they are different today from centuries ago.

Copyright © by Pearson Education, Inc. All rights reserved.

19 ▶ Comparing and Contrasting

Exercise 51

Critical Thinking

A. Choose one of the following systems: health care, public education, or child care. Write a paragraph describing the similarities and differences between the Scandinavian system and the system in the United States.

_____

_____

_____

_____

_____

_____

_____

_____

_____

B. Many people praise Scandinavia's social programs. Yet, there are those who do not favor a welfare state. Some of the following statements argue in favor of a welfare state. Some of the statements argue against a welfare state. Write *for* or *against* on the line before each statement.

_____ **1.** Scandinavians enjoy a high standard of living.

_____ **2.** Taxes are high in the Scandinavian countries.

_____ **3.** Sweden, Finland, Iceland, and Norway all have a literacy rate of about 99 percent.

_____ **4.** Medical care is available to all Scandinavians.

_____ **5.** The Scandinavian governments spend huge amounts of money on things the people could just pay for themselves.

Copyright © by Pearson Education, Inc. All rights reserved.

19 ▸ Identifying Reasons   Exercise 52

A. Choose the reason that best explains each statement. Circle the letter.

1. Scandinavia has little farmland because of

    a. volcanoes.   **b.** trade winds.   **c.** glaciers.

2. Iceland uses geothermal power because it has

    a. active volcanoes.   **b.** frequent hurricanes.   **c.** vast deserts.

3. Weather along the Scandinavian coasts is warmer than inland because of

    a. the North Atlantic Drift current.   **b.** trade winds.   **c.** volcanic activity.

4. In earlier times, the Vikings were feared throughout western Europe because

    a. they tried to force other people to accept their religion.   **b.** they raided other lands and stole property.   **c.** they were great traders.

5. Of all Scandinavians, about 99 percent can read because

    a. Scandinavians are smarter than other people in the world.   **b.** a public education is free to all Scandinavians.   **c.** Scandinavians who cannot read or write are put in jail.

B. Match each word with its definition. Write the letter beside the number.

_____ **1.** fjords   **a.** rocky islands

_____ **2.** skerries   **b.** long, detailed stories

_____ **3.** geothermal   **c.** huge sheets of ice that move slowly as they melt

_____ **4.** sagas   **d.** narrow bays surrounded by cliffs

_____ **5.** glaciers   **e.** energy from the heat of the Earth's interior

Copyright © by Pearson Education, Inc. All rights reserved.

19 ▶ Writing Poetically

A. A kenning is a descriptive phrase used in place of an everyday word or term. For example, a Viking poet might have used the following expressions:

- moon—"the night's lantern"
- snow—"the Earth's blanket"
- rain—"the gods' teardrops"

Choose at least two of the topics in the following box and describe them in your own kenning on the lines below.

sun	rain	dew	a ship
moon	a thunderstorm	snow	a star

_____

_____

_____

_____

B. Use an encyclopedia, another reference book, or the Internet to find information about Eric the Red or his son, Leif Ericson. Write a paragraph telling about the life of the one you chose. Describe his contribution to world history.

_____

_____

_____

_____

_____

_____

_____

_____

Copyright © by Pearson Education, Inc. All rights reserved.

20 ▷ Classifying Terms

Choose the correct category for each group of items. Circle the letter of that category.

1. Netherlands, Belgium

   a. high countries   **b.** low countries   **c.** Asian countries

2. Alps, Pyrenees, Apennines

   a. rivers   **b.** capital cities   **c.** mountain chains

3. Seine, Loire, Rhône, Danube

   a. mountains   **b.** sea ports   **c.** rivers

4. Lutheran, Methodist, Presbyterian, Baptist

   a. languages spoken in Switzerland   **b.** Roman Catholic churches   **c.** Protestant churches

5. Monet, Cézanne, Renoir

   a. religious reformers   **b.** French painters   **c.** German musicians

6. drachmas, francs, deutschmarks

   a. types of European currency   **b.** German sausages   **c.** styles of German clothing

7. steel, automobiles, machinery, electronics, chemicals

   a. main products of West Germany   **b.** main products of East Germany   **c.** main products of France

8. clothes, jewelry, perfume

   a. main products of Berlin   **b.** main products of Paris   **c.** main products of Prague

9. French, Swiss, German, Italian, Romansh

   a. the official languages of Italy   **b.** the official languages of France   **c.** the official languages of Switzerland

10. the modern organization that encourages free trade, promotes unity, uses the euro

    a. Common Market   **b.** European Union   **c.** European Community

Copyright © by Pearson Education, Inc. All rights reserved.

Name _____   Date _____

20 ▷ **Using a Map**   **Exercise 55**

Much of the Netherlands is below sea level. Mounds of earth called
dikes hold back the water and keep the sea from flooding the land.
Study the map below. Then answer the questions. You may use an
encyclopedia or the Internet.

The Netherlands

North
Sea

Amsterdam
Rotterdam

☐ Polders
▨ Sand plains
⬚ Southern uplands
■ Dunes
═ Dike
• City

1. The Dutch have created areas of rich farmland called *polders* by
pumping water into canals that flow into the North Sea. Find out
about two crops that are grown in these areas.

_____

_____

2. How was the water pumped into the canals when they were first
built? What method is used today?

_____

_____

3. Name a city built on a *polder*.

_____

4. A 20-mile-long dike separates a freshwater sea from what
saltwater sea?

_____

Copyright © by Pearson Education, Inc. All rights reserved.

20 ▸ Sequencing Events

Write the events in each of the following sets in the order in which they took place.

The Reformation

Martin Luther was thrown out of the Catholic Church.
Martin Luther argued against the practices of the Catholic Church.
Many Protestant denominations developed.

1. _____

2. _____

3. _____

The Reunification of Germany

The Berlin Wall was built separating East and West Berlin.
East and West Germany were reunited as Germany.
Germany was divided into East Germany and West Germany.

4. _____

5. _____

6. _____

The European Union (EU)

The EU introduced plans to have one system of money in 1999.
The Common Market became the twelve-member European Community (EC).
Several European governments set up an organization called the Common Market.

7. _____

8. _____

9. _____

Copyright © by Pearson Education, Inc. All rights reserved.

21 ▸ Comparing Nations

Exercise 57

Review

A. Which of the following statements describe characteristics shared by nations of Southern Europe? Circle the letters.

a. a dry climate

f. slow industrial development

b. rich, fertile soil

g. histories that go back to ancient times

c. poor, rocky soil

h. great wealth in comparison with Western Europe

d. dependence upon the sea

i. high-technology farming techniques

e. cold, wet winters

B. In 776 B.C., the Greeks held the first Olympic games. Today the Olympics are a modern tradition. The following statements describe the ancient Olympics. Compare these descriptions to today's games.

1. Athletes representing different groups came from all over Greece to compete in the games.

   _____

2. Only men competed in the ancient Olympics.

   _____

3. The earliest Olympic athletes wore no clothes when they competed in the games.

   _____

4. In ancient Greece, the winning athletes were awarded a crown of olive leaves.

   _____

5. The ancient Olympic games were held every four years.

   _____

6. The ancient Olympic games encouraged peace between nations.

   _____

Copyright © by Pearson Education, Inc. All rights reserved.

21 ▸ Classifying Civilizations

A. The items in the box began in the ancient civilizations of Southern Europe. Decide if each item is from the Greeks or from the Romans. Write each item under the correct heading.

democracy	building techniques	new ideas in science
modern drama	the Olympic games	a system of law

Greek   **Roman**

_____   _____

_____   _____

_____   _____

_____   _____

_____   _____

B. Use information from the chart. Circle the best answer.

Major Gods and Goddesses of Ancient Greece and Rome		
Description	**Greek name**	**Roman name**
King of the gods; lord of the sky	Zeus	Jupiter
Queen of the gods	Hera	Juno
God of the sea; brother of Zeus	Poseidon	Neptune
God of the underworld; brother of Zeus	Hades	Pluto
Goddess of love and beauty	Aphrodite	Venus
God of the sun	Apollo	Apollo
God of war	Ares	Mars
Messenger of the gods	Hermes	Mercury

1. The god (*Ares, Apollo*) was given the same name by the Greeks and Romans.

2. The planets of our solar system are named after (*Greek, Roman*) gods.

3. (*Zeus, Poseidon, and Hades* or *Hermes, Apollo, and Zeus*) are brothers.

4. Greeks with love problems would call upon (*Venus, Aphrodite*).

5. (*Hermes, Mercury*) would deliver messages to Jupiter.

Copyright © by Pearson Education, Inc. All rights reserved.

22 ▸ Interpreting a Quote

Exercise 59

Critical Thinking

A. Russia has been called a "geographer's paradise." After reading
Chapter 22, explain why that phrase might be used to describe Russia.

_____

_____

_____

_____

_____

_____

_____

B. Decide whether each statement is a *fact* (a statement that can be
proved true or false) or an *opinion* (a belief about something).
Write *F* or *O* beside each statement.

_____ **1.** Russia spans 11 time zones.

_____ **2.** Russia is the world's largest country.

_____ **3.** In Russia, one can meet fascinating and varied peoples.

_____ **4.** Russia's vastness and its many ethnic groups make it difficult to govern.

_____ **5.** Russia's economic and political future is uncertain.

_____ **6.** To promote goodwill and world peace, the United States should help
Russia's economic recovery.

_____ **7.** Mikhail Gorbachev was a Soviet leader.

_____ **8.** Moscow is the capital of Russia.

_____ **9.** Deposits of gold, iron, coal, tin, cobalt, copper, nickel, platinum, and
diamonds can all be found in Siberia.

_____ **10.** It is unfortunate that Siberia's harsh climate has kept Russia from
taking advantage of a wealth of natural resources.

Copyright © by Pearson Education, Inc. All rights reserved.

23 ▸ Using a Chart

Study the chart and answer the questions on the opposite page.

The Independent States of the Former Soviet Union: Selected Information		
State	**Population (approx.)**	**Characteristics**
Armenia	3,500,000	highly industrialized; limited natural resources and arable land; skilled, educated workforce; mainly Christian population
Azerbaijan	7,900,000	fertile land; ample oil; mainly Islamic population
Belarus	10,400,000	heavily industrialized; dependent on others for raw materials
Estonia	1,400,000	highly industrialized; skilled workforce; deposits of oil shale; one of the wealthiest of the states
Georgia	5,000,000	violent civil wars; well-educated population; warm climate; heavy tourism; exports wine and citrus fruits
Kazakhstan	16,800,000	huge nation; rich in natural resources; fine farmland; vast oil and mineral deposits
Kyrgyzstan	4,500,000	little oil or natural gas; some minerals and arable land; isolated from foreign markets; problems with ethnic rivalries
Latvia	2,400,000	in process of modernizing; heavy trade; problems with citizenship for Russian minority
Lithuania	3,600,000	a Roman Catholic nation; relies on nuclear reactors for majority of power; small minority population means little ethnic conflict
Moldova	4,500,000	was considered the "fruit basket" of the Soviet Union; good climate; fertile soil; strong ethnic conflicts
Russia	146,400,000	world's largest nation in area; relies on imports of food and clothing; has vast mineral wealth; main crops are grain and potatoes
Tajikistan	6,100,000	poorest state; highest rate of population growth; mainly agricultural; mainly Islamic
Turkmenistan	4,400,000	largely covered by Kara Kum Desert; cotton and natural gas main products; relies on import of food
Ukraine	49,800,000	huge nation; ample natural resources; grain exporter; heavy industry has caused pollution problems
Uzbekistan	24,100,000	Islamic state; cotton growers; natural gas reserves

Source: *The New York Times Almanac,* 2000

Copyright © by Pearson Education, Inc. All rights reserved.

23 ► Using a Chart (continued)

Exercise 60

Skill Practice

A. Read and answer the questions below.

1. Which states have the highest and lowest populations?

_____

_____

2. Which states have natural gas as a main product or in a reserve?

_____

_____

_____

3. List two states that have land that is good for farming.

_____

_____

4. List the state that must import its raw materials.

_____

_____

B. You are a newspaper reporter. You were sent to cover the breakup of the Soviet Union. Write a headline and news report that might have appeared in a newspaper on December 25, 1991—the official date of the end of the Soviet Union. You may write your report from the point of view of an American reporter or from the point of view of a Soviet reporter.

_____

_____

_____

_____

_____

_____

_____

Copyright © by Pearson Education, Inc. All rights reserved.

Name _____ Date _____

Today's papers or Web sites often report news from the 15 republics
that once comprised the Soviet Union. Find a story about current
events in one of the republics. Attach the article to this page.
Write a summary of the report on the lines below.

_____

_____

_____

_____

_____

_____

_____

_____

_____

_____

_____

_____

_____

_____

_____

_____

_____

_____

_____

_____

_____

Copyright © by Pearson Education, Inc. All rights reserved.

Name _____   Date _____

Compare the two maps. Then, complete the sentences below.

Eastern Europe, 1980s

Eastern Europe, 2000

1. East Germany and West Germany have become the single nation of

   _____ .

2. Czechoslovakia has become _____ and _____ .

3. What was once Yugoslavia has now become the nations of _____ ,

   _____ , _____ , and _____ .

Copyright © by Pearson Education, Inc. All rights reserved.

Name _____   Date _____

A. The following people played major roles in the twentieth-century history of Eastern Europe. Match each person with a nation. Then, select one person from this list. Write a brief description of that person's life. Tell how the person influenced events in that country. Use an encyclopedia or the Internet to find more information.

     1. Lech Walesa   **a.** Romania

     2. Tito   **b.** Poland

     3. Nicolae Ceausescu   **c.** Russia

     4. Mikhail Gorbachev   **d.** Yugoslavia

_____

_____

_____

_____

_____

_____

_____

_____

_____

_____

_____

_____

B. Find an article in a recent newspaper or on the Internet about one of the countries mentioned on this page. On a separate sheet of paper, write a summary of the article.

Copyright © by Pearson Education, Inc. All rights reserved.

Name_____ Date_____

A. Each of the following statements describes the geography of
Mongolia. Decide whether each statement belongs under the
category of *landforms*, *climate*, *human features*, or *economy*.
Write one category on the line following each statement.

1. Some Mongolians are nomadic herders who make their homes
   in movable tents. _____

2. The Gobi covers much of southern Mongolia. _____

3. Ninety percent of the people living in Mongolia are Mongols. _____

4. Mongolia's major trading partner is Russia. _____

5. Mongolia's chief exports are minerals. _____

6. Most of Mongolia has very little rainfall. _____

7. The country's official language is Mongolian. _____

8. Mongolia has changed from a nomadic, herding culture to a more
   agricultural and industrial one. _____

B. On another sheet of paper, write a few sentences that summarize the information that is shown on this pie graph.

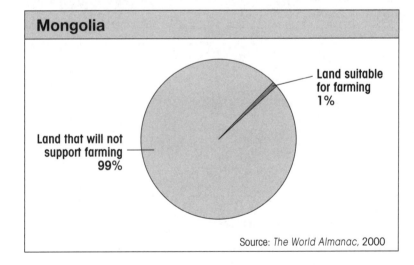

Copyright © by Pearson Education, Inc. All rights reserved.

25 ▶ Interpreting Cause and Effect

Exercise 65

Critical Thinking

A. Mongolia is the least densely populated country on the Earth.
Give three reasons why so few people live in Mongolia.

1. _____

2. _____

3. _____

B. Compare Mongolia's approximate population density with that of
some other nations by writing them in order of their population
per square mile. Begin with the nation with the lowest density.
End with the nation with the highest density.

Mongolia: 3 per sq. mi.   China: 337 per sq. mi.   Russia: 22 per sq. mi.

Japan: 865 per sq. mi.   United States: 73 per sq. mi.   Canada: 7 per sq. mi.

Mexico: 131 per sq. mi.   Vietnam: 530 per sq. mi.   Australia: 6 per sq. mi.

1._____   4._____   7._____

2._____   5._____   8._____

3._____   6._____   9._____

C. There is more livestock in Mongolia than there are people. Show
this fact on a bar graph by charting the following information.

human population: 2,247,000   sheep: 14,800,000   cattle: 2,200,000

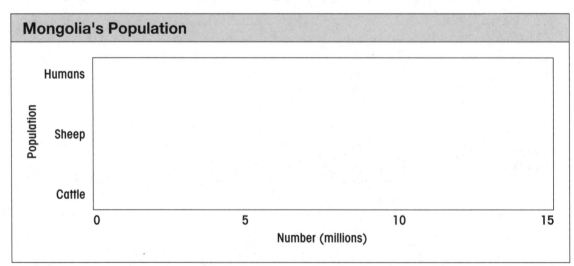

Copyright © by Pearson Education, Inc. All rights reserved.

Name _____ Date _____

The following graph illustrates China's population growth. Use information from the graph to select and circle the correct response to each item.

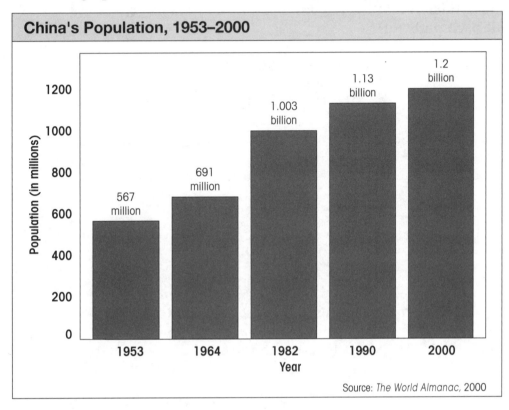

1. China's population has

   a. grown steadily.   **b.** decreased steadily.   **c.** risen and fallen.

2. In 1990, the United States census reported a population of nearly 249 million. That was

   a. more than the   **b.** slightly less than   **c.** much less than
   population   the population   the population
   reported for China.   reported for China.   reported for China.

3. According to the graph, no census figures were reported in China for the

   a. 1950s.   **b.** 1960s.   **c.** 1970s.   **d.** 1980s.

4. Based on the trend in this graph, which do you think would be true of China's population in the decade beginning in 2010?

   a. more than   **b.** about 2.1 billion people   **c.** about 1.4 billion
   3 billion people   people

Copyright © by Pearson Education, Inc. All rights reserved.

26 ▸ Studying Overpopulation

Exercise 67

Critical Thinking

A. Which problems would most likely stem from a rapid population growth in China? Which problems would most likely be the result of a declining population? Write *problem of growth* or *problem of decline* beside each problem.

_____ **1.** unemployment

_____ **2.** labor shortage

_____ **3.** higher taxes per person

_____ **4.** high percentage of older citizens

_____ **5.** food shortage

_____ **6.** housing shortage

B. Some of the problems listed above also are present in the United States. Choose one problem, and write a paragraph explaining how or whether the United States is trying to solve it.

_____

_____

_____

_____

_____

_____

_____

_____

_____

_____

_____

Copyright © by Pearson Education, Inc. All rights reserved.

26 ▸ Summarizing Facts About China   **Exercise 68**

A. Write two or three sentences that summarize each of the topics
listed below.

1. The teachings of Confucius

_____

_____

_____

2. Traditions of ancient China

_____

_____

_____

3. The economies of Taiwan and Hong Kong

_____

_____

_____

B. Write a two or three sentence answer to the situation below.

In 1989, Chinese students flooded Beijing's Tiananmen Square, calling for
democracy. The government silenced the protesters with tanks and guns.
Many students were killed. Hundreds were arrested. What do you think
would have happened if the Chinese government had not used force to halt
the demonstration and had allowed the protesters to have their say?

_____

_____

_____

_____

_____

_____

Copyright © by Pearson Education, Inc. All rights reserved.

Name _____   Date _____

**Read each summary of a newspaper article about Japan. In the
space below each summary, write a one-line headline for the article.**

1. From 1941: Japanese planes flew to the Hawaiian Islands, a
   state of the United States, and attacked the U.S. Navy fleet at
   Pearl Harbor. The attack destroyed 200 ships and angered the
   United States.

   _____

2. From 1947: The government of Japan voted today to give
   women living in Japan the same rights as men. These rights
   include the right to vote. Women who had been working
   for equal rights said the passage of the law was a victory.
   Others, who think women belong in the home, are unhappy
   with the law.

   _____

3. From 1952: Japan's economy has soared in recent years. This
   year, there has been an increase of 12 percent in the amount
   of goods made by factories in Japan. This increase in goods
   bought by other countries has helped Japan recover from
   World War II.

   _____

4. From 1995: An earthquake hit the Japanese city of Kobe.
   It was the most serious earthquake to hit Japan since 1923.
   More than 6,400 people were killed. Hundreds of thousands
   of people were left homeless.

   _____

5. From 1998: Japan's economy has had rough years lately.
   This year may be the worst yet. Many businesses have failed.
   Others are deeply in debt. The government is considering
   what measures to take to help the troubled economy.

   _____

Copyright © by Pearson Education, Inc. All rights reserved.

27 ▶ **Writing a Profile**

Exercise 70
Critical Thinking

You have been given the job of writing a profile of a Japanese woman engineer, the head of a large Japanese business, or a Kabuki actor. First, on another sheet of paper, write a list of questions that will help you to find important information about the way in which the person lives and what he or she is like. Then, fill out the graphic organizer below with answers the person might provide to your questions. Finally, on another sheet of paper, write the profile.

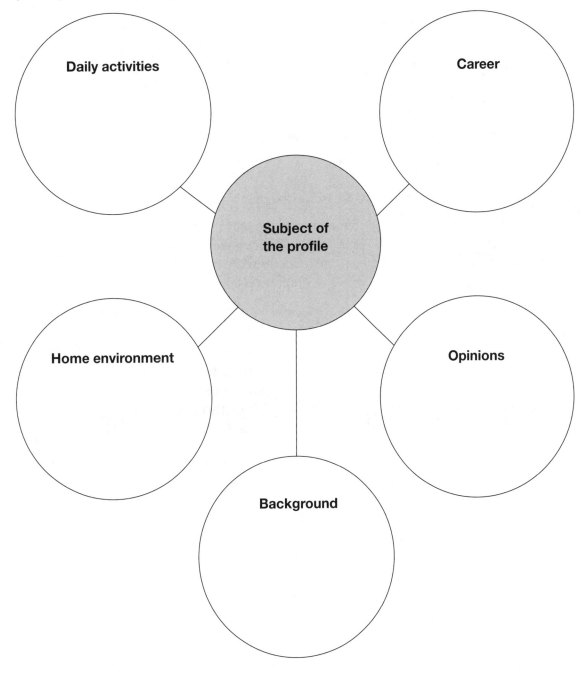

Copyright © by Pearson Education, Inc. All rights reserved.

27 ▷ Creating a Timeline

A. Listed below are some important events in Japan's history. Write the order in which they occurred. The first one has been done for you.

_____1_____ Japan enters World War II in 1941.

_____ In 1952, the United States leaves Japan after World War II.

_____ Women win the right to vote in 1947.

_____ By 1942, Japan's empire stretches from China to Myanmar.

_____ The United States drops the atomic bomb on Japan in 1945.

_____ In 1949, Japan's economy is growing rapidly.

B. Draw a line on the timeline and write where each event belongs. The first one is done for you.

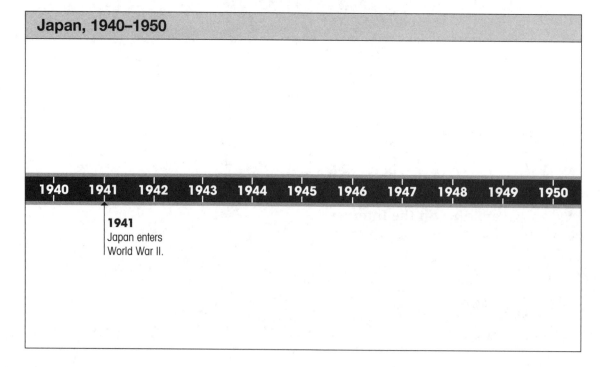

Japan, 1940–1950

| 1940 | 1941 | 1942 | 1943 | 1944 | 1945 | 1946 | 1947 | 1948 | 1949 | 1950 |

1941
Japan enters
World War II.

Copyright © by Pearson Education, Inc. All rights reserved.

Name_____ Date_____

A. Decide if each of the following statements describes North Korea
or South Korea. If you need help, use information in Chapter
28, or use an encyclopedia, an almanac, or the Internet. Write
the name of the country beside each statement.

_____ **1.** The country is run by a Communist government.

_____ **2.** This country has a strong capitalist economy.

_____ **3.** The capital city is Seoul.

_____ **4.** The capital city is Pyongyang.

_____ **5.** This country has one of the world's fastest-growing economies.

_____ **6.** This country imports and exports very little.

_____ **7.** This country is governed by Kim Dae Jung.

_____ **8.** This country is ruled by Kim Jong Il.

_____ **9.** It is also known as the Republic of Korea.

_____ **10.** It is also known as the Democratic People's Republic of Korea.

_____ **11.** After World War II, this country was occupied by Americans.

B. In the space below, sketch the flags of North Korea and South
Korea. You can find examples of the flags in an encyclopedia,
in an almanac, or on the Internet.

Copyright © by Pearson Education, Inc. All rights reserved.

Name_____ Date_____

Read and answer the following questions.

1. Do you think North Korea or South Korea would be a better place to live?

   _____

2. List four facts that you believe make the country that you selected a better place to live.

   _____

   _____

   _____

   _____

3. North and South Korea have discussed reunification. Do you think the two nations should become one again? Why or why not?

   _____

   _____

   _____

   _____

   _____

   _____

4. List two facts that support your opinion on reunification.

   _____

   _____

   _____

   _____

   _____

Copyright © by Pearson Education, Inc. All rights reserved.

Name _____ Date _____

Korea was one nation before World War II. Communists took over
the north in 1945, and North Korea and South Korea were formed
in 1948. Describe the social, political, and economic differences
between the two countries today.

_____

_____

_____

_____

_____

_____

_____

_____

_____

_____

_____

_____

_____

_____

_____

_____

_____

_____

Copyright © by Pearson Education, Inc. All rights reserved.

29 ▶ **Making a Graph**

A. Draw the bars on the graph below to compare India's population density with that of some other nations of the world. The bar for India has been drawn for you.

India: 788 per square mile

Mexico: 131 per square mile

United States: 73 per square mile

China: 337 per square mile

Japan: 865 per square mile

France: 280 per square mile

Australia: 6 per square mile

Russia: 22 per square mile

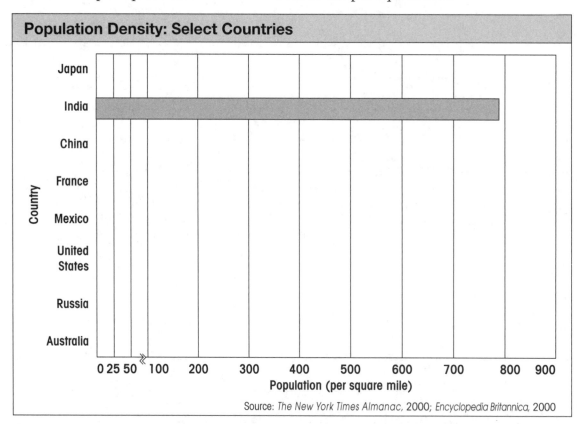

Source: *The New York Times Almanac, 2000; Encyclopedia Britannica, 2000*

B. From the information on the graph, circle the sentence that best summarizes India's population density in comparison with the other nations on the graph.

a. India is the second-most crowded country.

b. India is the most crowded country.

c. Mexico has more people than India.

d. Russia has more people than India.

Copyright © by Pearson Education, Inc. All rights reserved.

29 ▶ Identifying Fact and Opinion

Exercise 76

Review

A. Decide if each of the following statements is a *fact* or an *opinion*.
Write *F* if it is a fact. Write *O* if it is an opinion. Remember that
a statement of fact can be proved true or false. A statement of
opinion expresses a belief.

_____ **1.** India is the second-most populous country in the world.

_____ **2.** Only the People's Republic of China has more people than India.

_____ **3.** India should do something to limit its population growth.

_____ **4.** Someday, India will become the most populous country.

_____ **5.** More than 900 million people live in India.

_____ **6.** Of the people in India, 83 percent are Hindu.

_____ **7.** The Hindus should reject their traditional caste system.

_____ **8.** India is a democracy.

_____ **9.** Diamonds are found in India.

_____ **10.** India should make better use of its natural resources.

B. The following people played major roles in the history of India:
Mahatma Gandhi, Jawaharlal Nehru, Indira Gandhi. Choose one
of these people. Write a brief summary describing his or her life
and its effect on events in India. Use an encyclopedia or the
Internet to find information.

_____

_____

_____

_____

_____

_____

_____

_____

Copyright © by Pearson Education, Inc. All rights reserved.

30 ▸ Studying a Developing Nation

A. Agriculture is the most important economic activity in Bangladesh.
Eighty percent of the people in this country farm the land.
However, Bangladesh does not grow enough food for its large
population. Name the country's three main crops, and describe
three possible solutions to the problem of famine in Bangladesh.

_____

_____

_____

_____

_____

_____

_____

_____

B. Bangladesh has been struck with several natural disasters, including
monsoon rains, cyclones, and floods—a flood in 1998 stranded
more than 8,000,000 people. Few health services and poor
sanitation have resulted in poor drinking water and a very low
life expectancy. What could the world do to help Bangladesh?

_____

_____

_____

_____

_____

_____

Copyright © by Pearson Education, Inc. All rights reserved.

30 ▶ Classifying Information

A. Each of the following statements describes the geography of Pakistan or Afghanistan. Decide whether each statement belongs under the category of *landforms*, *climate*, *human features*, or *economy*. Write one category on the line following each statement.

1. Pakistan is one of Asia's poorest nations. _____

2. With a literacy rate of 26 percent, fewer than half of Pakistan's people can read and write. _____

3. The average worker in Pakistan makes about $340 a year. _____

4. Some of Pakistan's northern mountains are more than 22,000 feet high.

   _____

5. Punjabis make up Pakistan's largest ethnic group. _____

6. Afghanistan is mostly dry, with extreme temperatures. _____

7. More than 80 percent of Afghanistan's adults have had no formal schooling.

   _____

8. Afghanistan, a mountainous state with narrow passes, has been called "a narrow sword cut in the hills." _____

9. The majority of Afghanistan's population are Sunnite Muslim, and Islamic laws determine customs and lifestyles. _____

B. What do you think can be done to solve Pakistan's low literacy rate? On a separate sheet of paper, write three ideas.

Copyright © by Pearson Education, Inc. All rights reserved.

Name_____ Date_____

Use the map to complete the activities and questions below.

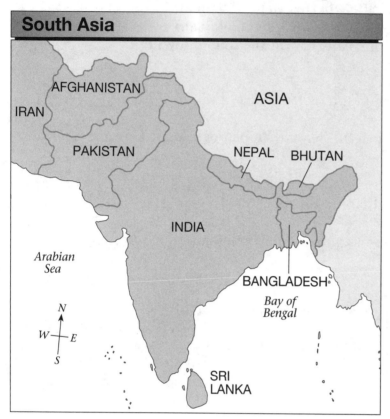

South Asia

1. In 1979, the Soviet Union invaded Afghanistan. In the eight-year war that followed, nearly 75 percent of Afghanistan's villages were damaged or destroyed, and 1.5 million people were killed. Millions of Afghans (25 percent of the population) fled over the mountains into Pakistan. The great number of refugees added to Pakistan's problems of overpopulation. Draw an arrow on the map to trace the movement of the Afghan refugees.

2. Is Afghanistan a landlocked nation or a coastal nation? _____

3. What sea does Pakistan border? _____

4. What nation borders Afghanistan to the west? _____

5. What nation borders Pakistan to the southeast? _____

Copyright © by Pearson Education, Inc. All rights reserved.

31 ▸ Interpreting a Story

Exercise 80

Critical Thinking

In Vietnam, a yearly monsoon brings violent winds and heavy rain. The following legend explains the climatic event. It also reflects the physical geography of the country with its many mountains and seacoasts. After you read the legend, circle the best answer to each question.

Why the Monsoon Comes Every Year

Over the years, many men had wanted to marry the beautiful Princess Mi Nuong. Yet, none had pleased her father, the emperor. One day, two suitors appeared at the same time. One man was called the Power of the Sea. The other was the Power of the Mountains. The emperor liked both men and could not choose between them.

"Whoever is the first to bring gifts to my daughter will become her husband," the emperor declared.

The Power of the Sea had his men gather pearls, tender squid, and juicy crabs. The Power of the Mountains used a magic wish book to fill a chest with emeralds and diamonds.

The Power of the Mountains returned to the palace first. He presented his gifts, and the emperor was pleased. Princess Mi Nuong married the Power of the Mountains.

When the Power of the Sea reached the palace, he found that he had lost the princess. He was very angry. He brought winds and rains. The ocean rose higher and higher. Giant waves rushed over the land. "Go after the Power of the Mountains!" he commanded his men. "Bring back Mi Nuong!" All the sea creatures became the army of the Power of the Sea. Wherever they ran, rivers flooded and people were killed.

The people of the villages prayed that the Power of the Sea would become calm again.

Finally, the Power of the Mountains took out his magic book. He opened it and asked that his mountain grow higher and higher. He took the Princess to the very highest peak. There, they were well out of the reach of the Power of the Sea.

When the Power of the Sea realized that his battle was pointless, he marched his men back to sea. The floods stopped, but the Power of the Sea was still very angry.

So it is that every year the Power of the Sea sends rushing waters and strong winds onto the land. He still hopes that he can get back the Princess for his bride.

For this reason, the monsoon comes each year to Vietnam.

---

1. What problems do the monsoons bring?

    a. drought   **b.** floods   **c.** sandstorms

2. How often do the monsoons occur?

    a. twice a year   **b.** once a year   **c.** once a decade

3. According to the legend, who controls the monsoons?

    a. the Power of the Mountains   **b.** the Power of the Sea   **c.** the Princess Mi Nuong

Copyright © by Pearson Education, Inc. All rights reserved.

31 ▸ Placing Events in Time

Decide during which time period each event occurred. Write *A*, *B*, or *C* on each line.

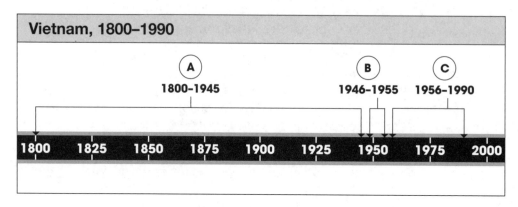

Vietnam, 1800–1990

| A | B | C |
| 1800–1945 | 1946–1955 | 1956–1990 |

1800 1825 1850 1875 1900 1925 1950 1975 2000

_____ **1.** In 1975, Saigon, the capital of South Vietnam, fell to the Communists.

_____ **2.** During World War II (1939–1945), Japan took Southeast Asia from France.

_____ **3.** The people of Southeast Asia defeated the French in 1954.

_____ **4.** Vietnamese Communists wanted to force French colonizers out of Vietnam, and fighting began in 1946.

_____ **5.** In 1945, at the end of World War II, France regained Southeast Asia.

_____ **6.** The United States, worried that communism would spread throughout Southeast Asia, became involved in Vietnam's conflict in the early 1960s.

_____ **7.** In 1957, Communist guerrilla fighters from the north began to try to take over South Vietnam.

_____ **8.** A 1954 conference in Geneva, Switzerland, divided Vietnam into two zones, with the Communists in control of the north.

_____ **9.** In 1965, President Lyndon Johnson sent more than 35,000 U.S. troops to Vietnam.

_____ **10.** In 1972, the United States took its troops out of Vietnam, but the war had not ended.

_____ **11.** During the 1800s, France took over the area of Southeast Asia that included Vietnam, Laos, and Cambodia.

Copyright © by Pearson Education, Inc. All rights reserved.

32 ► Studying Volcanoes

Exercise 82

Critical Thinking

Indonesia has about 60 active volcanoes. The largest eruption occurred in 1883 on the island of Krakatoa. The volcano collapsed to 1,000 feet below sea level, setting off a tsunami, or tidal wave, that killed 36,000 people in nearby Java and Sumatra. Use an encyclopedia or the Internet to help you answer the following questions about volcanoes.

1. How is a volcano formed?

_____

_____

_____

_____

_____

_____

2. What happens when a volcano erupts?

_____

_____

_____

_____

_____

_____

3. In spite of the destruction, volcanoes also produce benefits. For example, volcanic ash in Indonesia makes the soil fertile. What are three other benefits of volcanoes?

_____

_____

_____

_____

_____

Copyright © by Pearson Education, Inc. All rights reserved.

Name_____ Date_____

Critical Thinking

You live in a country described in Chapter 32. Respond to the following questions. Use information from your textbook and from the Internet.

Name of the country: _____

1. Do you live in an urban or rural area?

_____

2. Describe the climate.

_____

3. How does the climate affect your lifestyle?

_____

_____

4. Describe some of your religious or regional customs.

_____

_____

5. Describe some of the art, literature, music, or food of your region.

_____

_____

6. Describe either your occupation or the school that you attend.

_____

_____

7. If you had a visitor from another country, what sights would you take him or her to see?

_____

_____

8. What problems need to be solved in your homeland?

_____

_____

Copyright © by Pearson Education, Inc. All rights reserved.

Name_____ Date_____

A. Rewrite the following events in the order in which they occurred. Use **number one** for the earliest event.

  a. The Philippines proclaimed independence.
  b. Japan attacked the Philippines and occupied the islands during World War II.
  c. Ferdinand Marcos, the Philippine dictator, fled.
  d. Following the Spanish-American War, Spain sold the islands to the United States for $20 million.

  1. _____

  2. _____

  3. _____

  4. _____

B. Choose one of the events above, and write a summary of what happened.

  _____

  _____

  _____

  _____

  _____

  _____

  _____

  _____

  _____

  _____

  _____

Copyright © by Pearson Education, Inc. All rights reserved.

33 ▸ Identifying Fact and Opinion

Exercise 85

A *fact* is a statement that can be proved true or false. An *opinion* tells
what someone believes about something. A statement of opinion
often shows approval or disapproval. Decide whether each statement
is a fact or an opinion. Write *F* or *O* beside each statement.

_____ **1.** The Philippines are volcanic islands.

_____ **2.** The people of the Philippines probably worry about volcanic
eruptions every day of their lives.

_____ **3.** In 1991, Mt. Pinatubo erupted.

_____ **4.** The islands are swept by periodic typhoons.

_____ **5.** The Philippines is a very dangerous place to live.

_____ **6.** Manila Bay is the finest harbor in the Far East.

_____ **7.** The Philippine islands are located in sea lanes that link the western
Pacific and Indian oceans.

_____ **8.** Ferdinand Marcos ruled the Philippines for about 20 years.

_____ **9.** Marcos was a greedy man who spent his country's money on his own
personal pleasures.

_____ **10.** All but 5 percent of the population live on the five largest islands.

_____ **11.** Almost 75 percent of the population lives in poverty.

_____ **12.** It is unfair that there are a few very wealthy landowners in the
Philippines and so many people who are very poor.

_____ **13.** About 83 percent of the people in the Philippines are Catholic.

_____ **14.** The Philippines is the only Catholic nation in the region.

Copyright © by Pearson Education, Inc. All rights reserved.

33 Describing the Philippines

Exercise 86

Review

Write two paragraphs describing the physical geography and climate of the Philippines. Use at least five of the following words. Underline the words as you use them in your paragraph.

archipelago	Pacific Ocean	trade route	islands	typhoons
mountains	volcanic	Indian Ocean	Southeast Asia	

_____

_____

_____

_____

_____

_____

_____

_____

_____

_____

_____

_____

_____

_____

_____

_____

_____

_____

_____

_____

Copyright © by Pearson Education, Inc. All rights reserved.

Name _____ Date _____

Create a pie graph to represent each of the following statements.
A graph showing the percentage of Australians who work in
agriculture has been completed for you as an example.

1. Approximately 8 percent of Australia's
labor force is involved in agriculture.

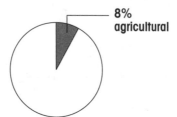

8%
agricultural

5. Approximately 89 percent of all
Australians can read and write.

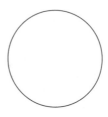

2. Approximately 11 percent of
New Zealand's labor force is
involved in agriculture.

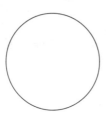

6. Approximately 99 percent of all
New Zealanders can read and write.

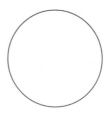

3. Only 6 percent of Australian land
is arable.

7. Australia's ethnic makeup is
approximately 95 percent European,
4 percent Asian and aboriginal.

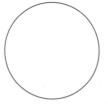

4. Only 2 percent of New Zealand's
land is arable.

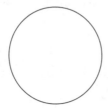

8. New Zealand's ethnic makeup is
approximately 81 percent European
(mostly British), 12 percent Polynesian
(mostly Maori), and 7 percent other.

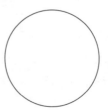

Copyright © by Pearson Education, Inc. All rights reserved.

34 ▸ Classifying Information

Exercise 88

Critical Thinking

Each of the following statements describes Australia or New Zealand or both. Decide whether each statement belongs under the category of *landforms*, *climate*, *human features*, or *economy*. Write one category on the line following each statement.

1. The 1,250-mile long Great Barrier Reef off Australia's northeast coast is the world's largest deposit of coral. _____

2. Australia's tallest mountain is 7,310-foot Mt. Kosciusko. _____

3. New Zealand is one of the world's leading exporters of wool.

   _____

4. Most New Zealanders take a strong antinuclear stand, and the country does not allow nuclear-armed or nuclear-powered vessels to use its port facilities.

   _____

5. The Maori of New Zealand have regained a sense of their culture and have become more successful. _____

6. Australia is the second driest continent on the Earth. (Antarctica is the driest.)

   _____

7. Australia is a close trading partner with Japan. _____

8. Most Australians speak English, but some speak a variety of aboriginal languages.

   _____

9. Both English and Maori are official languages of New Zealand.

   _____

10. New Zealand's two main islands are mostly hilly and mountainous while most of Australia is pancake-flat. _____

Copyright © by Pearson Education, Inc. All rights reserved.

Name _____ Date _____

Read each clue. Use information from your textbook and an
encyclopedia to match the clue to a term in the box. Write the
term where it belongs in the puzzle.

| Great Barrier Reef | aboriginal | Maori | koala |
| Great Dividing Range | sheep | kangaroo | |

Down

1. World's largest deposit of coral

Across

2. A long-leaping animal of Australia

3. The first peoples known to Australia

4. Australian animal that looks like a bear,
is often called a bear, but is not a bear

5. Australia's principal mountain chain

6. The first peoples known to New Zealand—
probably from Southeast Asia

7. In New Zealand, these animals outnumber
the people.

Copyright © by Pearson Education, Inc. All rights reserved.

35 ▸ Using a Map

Use information on the map to decide if the statements below are
true or false. Write *True* or *False* beside each number.

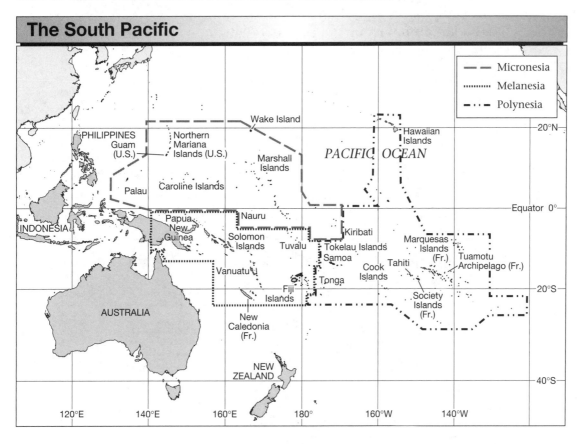

The South Pacific

_____ **1.** The Solomon Islands are located south of the equator.

_____ **2.** Tuvalu and Fiji are both located at a longitude of approximately
178 degrees.

_____ **3.** Nauru is located just north of the equator.

_____ **4.** The Marquesas Islands extend both north and south of the equator.

_____ **5.** The islands of Fiji are located at approximately the same latitudes as
the Northern Mariana Islands.

_____ **6.** Flying northeast from New Zealand, you would cross over the
Marshall Islands before crossing over Fiji.

_____ **7.** Flying east from Australia, you would reach New Caledonia before
reaching Polynesia.

Copyright © by Pearson Education, Inc. All rights reserved.

35 ▶ Planning a Trip

You are planning a trip to one of the islands of the Pacific. Use the travel section of a newspaper, call an airline or a travel agency, and use information in Chapter 35 to make your plans. You can also use an encyclopedia, an almanac, or the Internet. Outline your plans by addressing the items below.

1. Which island would you most like to visit? Give two reasons for your choice.

_____

_____

2. Describe your means of transportation.

_____

3. List your round-trip transportation costs.

_____

4. What would be the best time of year to visit this island? Why?

_____

5. What type of climate would you expect?

_____

6. Describe the lodging you would probably choose.

_____

_____

7. List sights you want to see.

_____

_____

8. List two recreational activities.

_____

_____

Copyright © by Pearson Education, Inc. All rights reserved.